THE TOP SECRET LIFE OF PLANTS

HOW PLANTS SURVIVE WILDFIRES

BY KATE MIKOLEY

Gareth Stevens
PUBLISHING

Please visit our website, www.garethstevens.com. For a free color catalog of all our high-quality books, call toll free 1-800-542-2595 or fax 1-877-542-2596.

Library of Congress Cataloging-in-Publication Data

Names: Mikoley, Kate, author.
Title: How plants survive wildfires / Kate Mikoley.
Description: New York : Gareth Stevens Publishing, [2020] | Series: The top secret life of plants | Includes index.
Identifiers: LCCN 2018030203| ISBN 9781538233894 (library bound) | ISBN 9781538233870 (paperback) | ISBN 9781538233887 (6 pack)
Subjects: LCSH: Plants–Adaptation–Juvenile literature. | Plants–Effect of fires on–Juvenile literature.
Classification: LCC QK912 .M55 2019 | DDC 581.4–dc23
LC record available at https://lccn.loc.gov/2018030203

First Edition

Published in 2020 by
Gareth Stevens Publishing
111 East 14th Street, Suite 349
New York, NY 10003

Copyright © 2020 Gareth Stevens Publishing

Designer: Sarah Liddell
Editor: Abby Badach Doyle

Photo credits: Cover, p. 1 KarenHBlack/Shutterstock.com; glass dome shape used throughout bombybamby/Shutterstock.com; leaves used throughout janniwet/Shutterstock.com; background texture used throughout MInerva Studio/Shutterstock.com; p. 5 (oxygen) suwan supavasit/Shutterstock.com; p. 5 (fuel) Vasilyev Alexandr/Shutterstock.com; p. 5 (heat) John D Sirlin/Shutterstock.com; p. 5 (wildfire) S. Borisovich/Shutterstock.com; p. 7 Lucky-photographer/Shutterstock.com; p. 9 (South African aloe) Victoria Field/Shutterstock.com; p. 9 (Australian grass tree) A Moment In Time/Moment Open/Getty Images; p. 11 Karel Stipek/Shutterstock.com; p. 13 Sundry Photography/Shutterstock.com; p. 15 William Campbell/Contributor/Corbis News/Getty Images; p. 17 (fire lilies) Artesia Wells/Shutterstock.com; p. 17 (blowtorch) Nadia Brusnikova/Shutterstock.com; p. 19 MayumiKataoka/Wikimedia Commons; p. 21 Smileus/Shutterstock.com.

Printed in the United States of America

CPSIA compliance information: Batch #CS19GS: For further information contact Gareth Stevens, New York, New York at 1-800-542-2595.

CONTENTS

Words in the glossary appear in **bold** type
the first time they are used in the text.

HARMFUL AND HELPFUL

In nature, fires can take over large areas and destroy everything in their path. These events, called wildfires, happen in many **environments,** from forests to fields. Wildfires can leave areas completely bare!

It may seem that wildfires are only harmful to the world around them. But for some **ecosystems,** wildfires are important. They give **nutrients** back to the soil and remove plants that could harm new growth. Some plant **species** have ways to survive wildfires—and some even depend on them!

CLASSIFIED!

MOST WILDFIRES ARE CAUSED BY PEOPLE, THROUGH ACTIVITIES SUCH AS BURNING CAMPFIRES IN UNSAFE AREAS. HOWEVER, SOME WILDFIRES ARE CAUSED BY EVENTS IN NATURE, SUCH AS LIGHTNING.

ALL FIRES NEED THREE THINGS TO BURN: HEAT, OXYGEN (AIR), AND **FUEL**. FIREFIGHTERS TRY TO REMOVE AT LEAST ONE OF THESE THINGS TO STOP A WILDFIRE.

THE FIRE TRIANGLE

OXYGEN

fire

FUEL

HEAT

5

CHANGING TO SURVIVE

Over time, plants and animals go through changes that help them live better in certain environments. These changes are called adaptations. Many plants have adapted to survive wildfires.

When a fire is coming, animals can run or crawl away to stay safe. Plants can't do that, so they depend on their adaptations to help. One fire adaptation common in trees is thick bark. Thick bark acts as insulation, which means it's strong enough to block the fire from killing the tree.

CLASSIFIED!

SEQUOIAS ARE VERY LARGE TREES THAT OFTEN GROW IN CALIFORNIA. THEIR BARK CAN BE UP TO 2 FEET (61 CM) THICK! A SEQUOIA'S BARK CAN BE BURNED BY FIRE, BUT THE TREE CAN STAY ALIVE.

GIANT SEQUOIAS CAN LIVE FOR THOUSANDS OF YEARS, EVEN THOUGH THEY GROW IN AREAS WHERE WILDFIRES ARE COMMON.

7

LEAF PROTECTION

Some plants don't have thick bark—or any bark at all—to save them from wildfires. Instead, their leaves help keep them safe.

When leaves die, many plants simply drop them to the ground. Other plants hold on to their dead leaves for a sneaky way to outsmart wildfires. The old leaves pack together around the plant's stem to keep it safe from the fire's heat. Australian grass trees and South African aloes are examples of plants that survive wildfires this way.

WHEN A PLANT PROTECTS ITSELF FROM HEAT AND FIRE WITH THICK BARK OR DEAD LEAVES, IT'S CALLED THERMAL INSULATION.

South African aloe plant

Australian grass tree

AN UNDERGROUND SECRET

After a fire goes through some places, it may look like all the plants in the area have burned and died. But beneath the ash and dirt, some plants are hiding a sneaky secret. Sometimes, the parts above ground that you can see may be destroyed...but underground, these plants are just fine! The soil acts as insulation to protect their roots and other underground plant parts.

CLASSIFIED!

SOME PLANTS HAVE A WOODY UNDERGROUND PART CALLED A LIGNOTUBER (LIHG-NOH-*TOO*-BER). THE LIGNOTUBER HAS FOOD AND OTHER THINGS TO HELP THE PLANT GROW AGAIN—EVEN AFTER THE TOP HAS BEEN DESTROYED!

Some **herbs** have special underground bulbs or stems. After a fire, they will **sprout** new growth.

BANKSIA IS A KIND OF PLANT THAT COMMONLY SURVIVES FIRES BECAUSE OF ITS LIGNOTUBER.

A TALL
CROWN

Some trees keep most of their leaves and branches very high up in what's called the crown. Trees that do this, such as some Eucalyptus and pine species, have long, mostly bare trunks. When a wildfire comes, the trunks may become burned, but the fire is less likely to reach the leaves and branches.

Some trees have even adapted to "self-prune." This means they're able to remove branches that have died and could act as fuel

CLASSIFIED!

OLDER, LARGER TREES OFTEN SURVIVE WILDFIRES BECAUSE OF THEIR ADAPTATIONS. HOWEVER, SEEDLINGS, OR YOUNG TREES, OF THE SAME SPECIES MAY DIE BECAUSE THEY'VE NOT YET GROWN STRONG ENOUGH.

PONDEROSA PINE TREES HAVE A TALL CROWN AND SELF-PRUNE. THEY CAN LIVE TO BE HUNDREDS OF YEARS OLD!

SUPER-SEALED SEEDS

Some plants are able to survive in spite of wildfires. Other plants need fires to spread seeds and stay alive! A type of tree called the lodgepole pine grows in areas where wildfires happen.

Lodgepole pines have cones that are naturally sealed with **resin**. Seeds can only come out when the resin has melted. When a wildfire comes through, it melts the resin, allowing the cone to open and spread its seeds. Soon, a whole new group of trees will grow!

CLASSIFIED!

IN ORDER FOR A LODGEPOLE PINE'S CONE TO RELEASE ITS SEED, ITS RESIN NEEDS TO REACH AT LEAST 113°F (45°C)!

WILDFIRES MAY KILL INDIVIDUAL LODGEPOLE PINES, BUT THEY'RE IMPORTANT FOR HELPING NEW GROWTH.

RISING FROM THE ASH

Sometimes different kinds of plants can help each other. When the plants that can't survive wildfires are burned up, they turn into ash. Ash acts as a **fertilizer** to soil, so after a harmful fire, some plants produce beautiful flowers!

The Australian grass tree is known for its big spikes. After a fire, these spikes quickly pop up—often the first sign of survival. When grown outside of the wild, people sometimes use blowtorches to help these plants **bloom**!

SOME KINDS OF FIRE LILY CAN ONLY GROW FLOWERS AFTER FIRES.

fire lilies

CLASSIFIED!

SURPRISINGLY, SOON AFTER A WILDFIRE, THE AFFECTED AREA CAN BECOME COVERED IN FLOWERS. SOME PLANTS CAN FLOWER AS SOON AS 9 DAYS AFTER A FIRE!

blowtorch

BLOOMING
AGAIN

Buds are small parts of a plant that will eventually grow into a new flower, branch, or leaf. You can often see buds on the outside of plants before they bloom.

Some species of Eucalyptus, however, keep their buds hidden! The buds on these trees are protected under the bark of the trunk. If the tree gets burned in a fire, the buds will come out from under the burned bark. Now they can bloom into new leaves or branches!

THOUGH SOME EUCALYPTUS TREES HAVE ADAPTED TO HELP THEIR SPECIES SURVIVE FIRE, THE TREES' SAP AND BARK IS ACTUALLY QUITE **FLAMMABLE!**

21

GOOD OR BAD?

In some places, wildfires happen as often as every 5 years. In other places, there may be hundreds of years between one fire and the next! When wildfires are started by people, they can happen more often.

Wildfires can be harmful, but they're also important to help new growth happen. That's why in some areas, if the fire is not a danger to people, it's left to burn naturally. That helps new plants grow so the whole ecosystem can benefit.

CLASSIFIED!

A FIRE HAS TO BE JUST RIGHT FOR SEEDS TO SPREAD. PLANTS WON'T GROW BACK IF A FIRE IS TOO BIG, TOO HOT, OR BURNS TOO LONG.

WITHOUT WILDFIRES, MANY FORESTS WOULD NOT BE ABLE TO GROW NEW TREES.

21

GLOSSARY

bloom: to produce flowers

ecosystem: all the living things in an area

environment: the natural world in which a plant or animal lives

fertilizer: something added to the soil that helps plants grow

flammable: something that can be set on fire and will burn quickly

fuel: something that is burned to make energy, heat, or power

herb: a low-growing plant used to add flavor to food

nutrient: something a living thing needs to grow and stay alive

resin: yellow or brown sticky stuff, made by some kinds of trees

species: a group of plants or animals that are all of the same kind

sprout: to grow or to produce new leaves or buds

FOR MORE INFORMATION

BOOKS

Furgang, Kathy. *Wildfires*. Washington, DC: National Geographic, 2015.

Long, Erin. *Plants and Their Environments*. New York, NY: PowerKids Press, 2017.

Spilsbury, Louise and Richard. *Top 10 Worst Wildfires*. New York, NY: PowerKids Press, 2017.

WEBSITES

Earth Science for Kids: Forest Fires
www.ducksters.com/science/earth_science/forest_fires.php
Read more about how forest fires start and spread.

Fires in Nature
smokeybear.com/en/about-wildland-fire/benefits-of-fire/fire-in-nature
Learn about where wildfires happen in the United States.

Playing with Wildfire: 5 Amazing Adaptations of Pyrophytic Plants
www.britannica.com/list/5-amazing-adaptations-of-pyrophytic-plants
This page has more facts on how some plants survive wildfires.

23

INDEX